SHEDDING

the necessity and capacity of forgetting

By

Rhys Daly

ACKNOWLEDGEMENTS

For so many people including, but not limited to, the following. For Joy, Nen, and Mani, who never treated me like a child. For Jeff and Sara who taught me to not be afraid of my art. For Myles, a young professor who told me he enjoyed my writing and hoped I would continue. And for Lizzie who, after I had completely ignored Myles' very kind words and stopped writing entirely for years, got drunk with me and came up with the crazy idea that maybe I should start writing again and tell people about it.

Thank you. I will always cherish your wit and wisdom.

CONTENTS

THE WOODS

THE CRACKS

MANY HAPPY ONES

SHEDDING

SKIN

OCEANOGRAPHY AND OTHER PASTIMES

Are you ready to rip into a stranger's skin
because I'm bored?

I've hoarded my fingernails
in a Mason jar
and stuck them into my fists
so they look like
keratin sea urchins.

Are you ready to rip into my skin?

HOLD IT

Hold it.

When was the last time you pissed yourself?

You've never been truly hungry before,
not in any way that counts,
a stomach pang is nothing
if your coat is worth a mother's hands.

The mannequin works harder than you do,
it knows a heart in pieces may heal with time
but a fragmented brain
requires more than waiting to be cured.

What kind of five-year-old knows you can't be resuscitated
from head trauma?

Hold it.

What's Undone

There's a less-than-peaceful protest
inside my skin.

I find someone has taken
chainsaws to my bones,
cutting open growth plates,
un-fusing,
undoing all my work
until I feel growing pains.

They remind me of the times
when I had eyes
that viewed me as immaculate.

PERSPECTIVES AND SECOND OPINIONS

When I looked hard into the mirror
I could see the spiders in my eyes
feeding on my memories,
unwinding my irises into
double helixes
that code for a pair of cameras
projecting a movie
of memories
about the time I spent
in the cracks where I grew up.

With my three views intertwined
I could see a single vision
with more perspective.

I appreciate the gesture,
but I don't think that's what spiders
are supposed to do.

FOR WHEN I GET OUT OF HERE

The spiders in your eyes aren't doing their job.

They've eaten each other's legs
and have left you with a skull full of spider bodies
that rattles when you shake it.

My spiders still have their legs
but are too busy constructing
cameras with them
to do much else.

Neither of us move.

At least not forward.

You are mostly just pushed around in circles in your chair,
and I mostly just spin in circles in mine
and watch the bird on my wall.

It doesn't have a body, head, or legs,
so its wings pull against nothing
as it struggles towards me.

I pick it up.

I throw the bird against the wall
to see if it will grow legs and walk away.

I throw my chair against the wall
to see if it will sprout wings and fly.

I throw my head against the wall
to see if I can make the spiders crawl out of my ears
and carry my head back to me.

I think that would be interesting.

Instead, they leave their imprints on the walls
and all three
land,
stuck together into one thing
that stares at me.

An upside-down creature
with the thin wooden legs of a chair,
the feathers of a crow,
and the head of my head.

I stare at my head, then at you,
and hope my eyes don't look as dead as yours.

WHAT'S THE NAME OF YOUR TAILOR?

You look like someone's wearing
your skin today.

Your movement's off,
you've bent your arm in a way
unfamiliar.

I think you crawled
out of your mouth
and handed your skin to a stranger to pilot.

Someone unconcerned with appearances
who seems more comfortable in your jacket
than you do
so you could have a day off
from being someone else.

BINOCULARS WON'T HELP

When you're your own voyeur
viewing your experiences,
pleasures of the past,
as you're suspended in branches of a flower bush,
expecting a blush and rush of life,

and instead
find that from afar,
made abstract by time and distance,
they're alarming,

you'll gouge out your eyes
with thorns from the vines you're entwined in
and stuff the sockets
with flower petals to rose tint
that hint of unhappiness welling within you.

An Error in Transcription

Touching sheer
is someone watching you struggle to stay cordial
when you answer the paper-cup-telephone
you made when you were seven,
and on the other end of the line
are cotton friends
whose names you've forgotten.

Touching sheer
is knowing the rainbow cords in their eyes are unordered,
but not recalling their proper places
or how you would even begin to braid them
before they coil themselves together
and settle into piles at your feet.

Touching sheer
is capturing the event in your eyelids
and feeling like the subtle grooves
in your frenzied sketches
are more reality
than the reality they sadly attempt to reflect.

Touching sheer
is keeping careful record

each time you pass through old existences,
moments you struggle to conjure with open eyes
now that your only clarity
is a hole in the drywall.

FRESH PEELS

Don't pick at the holes in the walls
of your dreams.

And close your eyes
when there's blood around,
because I've found that scabs,
even in memory,
have a tendency to gush
and you don't want to accidentally recognize something

red.

LENS

There's something crawling in my throat
and something else
(not a spider)
in my eyes.

It feels like skin,
an extra pair of eyelids that are too big
and in the back.

They have a memory
stamped on the inside
that tints my vision
with something from the woods.

I HAVE A QUESTION

Some part of me is wrapped in branches,
but I'm not sure which limb,
or if it's a different sort of extremity.

If I run and trip
or a piece of me rips
off,
I'll know what part was trapped.

AND AN ANSWER

If I could grow another limb
it would be
a left arm.

Or antlers.

A SERIES
OF GOINGS

If I were a tree
I'd be less afraid of
when my feet won't move.

Or when my arms
fall off.

Or when the skin from my fingers
peels away
and I lose all my hair.

If I were a tree,
I don't know why yet,
but I'm sure I'd learn to be afraid
of the sounds
from my fingers.

If I were a tree…

When I turn orange like the leaves,
please take what liquid you can find
from the sap of someone else
and paint me another color
before showing off my body
in that museum you're always
going on about.

Or…

To keep my body calm
embalm me in something
stronger than formaldehyde
and wood alcohol.

Reorganize my organs into convenient
half-quart jars
and sew my skin with my hair into a quilt
stuffed with memories
so I can carry them with me
when I go into the woods again.

But please...

Allow my first four metatarsals
to be morsels for bacteria.

My marrow
a feast for worms and blowflies.

Eyes and tongue a home
for maggots and other hordes,
and then maybe
my mind will be consumed
by something more than words.

But…

When I taste your skin again,
I'll know I want it to choke me
so
I'll steal your hand to replace my tongue,
and use it to pull you in.

You'll fashion a knife from one of my floating ribs
and use it to cut your way out.

As you writhe away
you'll cut your hand from my mouth with my rib
which you then return to me
plunging it into the wound where you found it.

And it will always seep.

I know you'll stay here
lapping it up
carefully kissing all the blood back into me.

And I cannot ask you to stop
for your hand, my tongue, is in my side,
and my rib, your hand, is ours.

The taste of your skin will be washed out by my blood.

And I will miss it.

So...

Skewer me on the steeple of a church.

Run ropes of my insides down the spire into the belfry
toll the bell with my intestines
light lanterns with the oils
collected from my pores.

Drain everything from me
to let my body become like marble
and use every bit of my pigment to paint cathedral ceilings
depicting something
looking like the birds I see in my head
from Revelation
or Ezekiel
wheels and wings they never taught me in Sunday school.

Unscroll my tongue
and let me speak the name of that angel with four faces
and his truths they did not let me know.

If you do it fast enough,
I may enjoy evisceration
for
my last moments will be filled with tolling bells
and terrifying words
like I always wanted.

And I'll finally be ready...

When I fly to Jericho,
know I'll never touch the stones
again.

Float my belongings
across the Mediterranean
towards my mother,
and light them
when they reach Carthage.

See the procession of my pyre,
admire how it all becomes as black
as I imagined it to be
in life.

But unlike me,
their char will fertilize the earth,
watch them
nourish snails that will clothe
royalty
when they all fly to Jericho
like me.

So...

When my antlers are untangled
and I reach
the top of this hill in the wood,
I'll know exactly how far I grew.

I'd like to be able to see forever
and know I'll never be asked
to travel the divide,
live to see infinity
and know I'll never have to fill the gaping hole
that is the world.

Because a mile alone is paralyzing,
like analyzing
the yellow-red eyes
that stare back at me
when I look back into my old kitchen
in the woods.

THE
THINGS
THAT
WENT

Didn't I Know You?

There's a clever little creature
in the corner of the kitchen
winding strings of stars around its horns
for reasons unknown to me.

And though the burning strings
illuminate the darkened room,
their lights seem dim
compared to the twinkle
in the creature's eyes.

The twinkles water cacti with tequila
and no matter how hard I shine my light
I cannot put the vacuum away.

Those eyes are burnt around the edges
but searing in the iris,
like I'm looking over a ledge into
the brightest abyss
I've ever seen,
wondering
if this is the light at the end of the tunnel
you're always going on about.

RODS AND CONES

Can you see it?

The thing
behind the wall of light?

If you're willing to let your irises be bleached by heat,
you might sneak a peek
at the thing.

You can let it burn there,
then blink away the rings
until you're ready to stare again.

If you're willing.

Because the flashes of light
you see when you blink
after staring
and holding your breath too long
just might be
salvation.

A Staggering Lack of Milk

Everywhere is China
if you've never seen the sun.

And like the man in the apartment building opposite,
whose window with half-opened shades
are so close and low enough
I can see the hair on his inner thighs,
I was never taught the recipe
for porcelain.

In which direction do your knees sway?

I doubt they are predictable.

Who is that screaming at us from far away?

I hope they bring their own beers.

Rip apart your seams if you have any,
and become your bedside ragdoll.

If I ever leave this room,
would I discover I am only what's been jettisoned,

only powder from the fingertips of the owner of those thighs,
wafting through the stowaway rays
that sneak in through his windows?

SHE READ ROAD SIGNS OUT LOUD

My mother was a seagull.

She taught me old sayings
that may or may not have been true,
things like,

It's always a step sideways to murder.

Or,

*Run like the edge of this cliff
is where you have always belonged.*

Were our toes as rough as we always believed they were?

Even if they weren't,
I knew she could drag a reverie
from every stone on this mountain
if she were larger than the orange splotches
that remain in my eyes
when I look at the things that scare me most.

SHUTTER NOISES ARE RELICS

Take a crapshoot snapshot
of the thing making footstep noises
as it passes by you between the trees every month or so.

Catch the crunches on camera
and you might just see
what goes bump in the night,
you'll know what the monster
in your closet always looked like.

But it's not a frightening type of enlightenment.

Just a kind that flies by
to remind you
of how slow you're going.

COLLAPSING LUNGS

Do you hear that?

The sound of no one breathing?

The sound of breath collectively held
in anxiety
or
anticipation.

We will not know which until we open our mouths
and scream
or
speak
in unison.

THE SOUND THAT FINGERS MAKE

The willow tree fingers are locusts
that many plagues ago
stripped the branches bare.

They hang on the skeleton
and mourn what they destroyed.

They pay their penance
by replacing what once was,
quaking
and hissing
when a breeze passes through them.

From afar you'd never know the tree is dead.

SHE'LL REMIND YOU WHAT YOU SAW IN THERE

There's a bird out there who has your soul.

Her pitch-black eyes were with you
in the womb as your skin grew
and your hair fell out.

Body-less, her eyes were yours
until the day you spoke your first real word.

Her eyes caught the word and they rolled out of your skull
to find her body out in the woods
where the word will remain
in her eyes
until the day you meet.

If you ask her the question
your first word will answer,
she'll return your soul
and you'll finally feel like you can see clearly
for the first time since you spoke.

CENTERED

What if we stood in the center
of a circle
and waved at the passersby
with branches?

Just you and me?

And something sort of frightening
if you look at it too hard?

Something we picked up from the streets?

The three of us holding hands
and standing,
watching,
waving
from the center of a circle
at the stream of skin from my scalp
spiraling
into the woods?

THE
WOODS

RERUNS

I forgot how much it rains here in the woods.

It stings more than I remembered.

I'm not sure when I left here
or how all my skin is gone
except in the places
where my fingers
touch in fists
clenching the ribbons of my flesh,

but I think I hear something
familiar.

IT ALL SMELLS LIKE CHERRIES

Water droplets are filled with words
in languages
I wish I'd learned.

Entire streams of Spanish,
sounds my tongue never learned to produce,
rivers of noise I'd love to jump into
that run surprisingly like the lines
in my grandmother's palms.

She taught me to swim
by throwing me into the river
and shouting

Swim!

I wonder if I still know how.

WHEN DID YOU GET SO TALL?

Emerging from the woods
something with the brittle legs of a baby deer.

He has a familiar face,
I think it was childhood friend,
so I asked him,

Don't I know you?

He responded with a tap of a hoof
and a shake of his familiar head.

But I know it's you,
Old Friend.

Didn't I tell you I'd be returning to the woods?
I'm sorry I came back unrecognizable.

You turn away and head back through,
already grown into a stag.

I wonder how I missed our childhood.

There Was No Admission Fee

The stag has brought me to the museum
he's always going on about.

He hid it deep in the woods
and refurbished it over the years.

He filled it with so many things
that when looked at sideways,
I manage to have a vague remembrance of.

I'd like to remember them even when I've left.

I'll do my best to sketch them.

THE ENTRYWAY

There's a brochure in the entryway.

It reads:

If you're looking hard enough
you'll find
The Hotel of Sound,
a monument of memories to
moments
momentarily forgotten.

Stare into the sonogram
and open up the door.

You may just hear
your first breath
if you listen very closely.

Performance Art

A wasp is chewing up
the rafters
of my grandparents' house
to construct a paper nest.

It's dangled from the center of the ceiling.

She's buzzing around it,
wondering where all the candles came from,
reprimanding me for tracking
wet footprints
through the lobby.

AND THE RAZOR NEVER DULLS

Someone's standing in the center of the room
shaving their head.

The clippings fall into a bowl of milk.

They're screaming about how it gives them courage.

The hair grows back faster than they can cut it.

On a Pedestal In An Otherwise Blank Room

An insect,
pink
as artificially dyed candy.

The shell opened,
revealing the candy color through and through.

Its laboratory watermelon legs and antennae
prodding the pedestal.

It reminded me of
my old candy shell,
once painted shining red
with remnants
of its cousins' exoskeletons
collected by bloody child-mica-miner fingers,
and some chemical that causes cancer
according to the state of California.

Blood, sweat, and tears that lacquered me
until I felt like I was something stronger.

I Can't See Him, But I Know He's Here Somewhere

My wet shoes squeak out harmonies
to the music of the bagpiper
playing in the vents.

It's a victory dance
you're meant to do
on a spiked shield
over your enemy's corpse.

The floor is littered with books and movies
I used to love.

WHY DID YOU BRING ME HERE?

The stag and I have found
light leaking from
the cracks
in the walls of a familiar room.

They're fairly narrow.

We can only look inside
by pressing our eyes
against the walls.

I hear a multitude of voices
clearly
in many languages.

They're telling me to climb the stairs
on all fours,
and asking questions
about things I hardly remember
from the hazy childhood that plays before me.

THE
CRACKS

Head down.
It says,
Put your head down.
The wheels are whores,
I'm not a hero for those
who have forgotten how to finger paint,
and the beetle in my pocket says,

Put your head down.
The smoking corner is a pharmacy,
I've never remembered what kind of tree
dropped all these seeds,
and the beetle in my pocket says,

Put your head down.
The wind chimes are snakes,
I remember that Chinese calligraphy
is composed of many ordered strokes,
and the beetle in my pocket says,

Put your head down.
My eyes have expanded,
but I will never know the fate
or color of the fish who dreams of walking,
because the beetle in my pocket insists,

Keep your head down,
down deep in your pocket.

It says,
keep your head down.

How feral are the remaining memories
in the cracks where you grew up,
and could you tame them all again
if they caught a whiff
of drying pottery?

I am a child
in a field on Easter Sunday.

My basket's full of
torn up grass,
I'm jumping off rocks,
and my kneecaps are missing.

A shadow looks on disapprovingly
at my fingers laced into another child's.

The stag asks me if the other child is a boy or girl.

I remember someone telling me
we can only float so freely
as the bones inside our knees.

I tell the stag,

I don't think it matters.

What sorts of waterbugs
still creep in the cracks
where you grew up,
and do they remember
your name
or the color of your bedroom walls?

I'm placing a sculpture
on my nightstand.

I want it to watch me sleep.

Fingers stained, hair matted by paste,
I stand proudly,
transfixed
by my glittery, blue, papier- mâché
egg,
inscribed:

My name's inside!
It's full of spiders!

A shadow passes behind me.

God, that's creepy.

Who else was with you
in the cracks where you grew up,
and why was the last time
you saw them
your brother's birthday?

A tune like happy birthday,
but in a minor key,
haunts the spice cupboard
and forces me to sing along as I cook dinner.

My younger brother doesn't breathe,
he seizes and stays silent for years
so I never try to talk to him.

selfish

The shadow cries the first time my brother speaks.

How many other eyes
have pried apart the panels
that mask the cracks
where you grew up,
and do you mind that they were watching
your first kiss?

My tongue's entwined with a face I cannot recognize.

Someone's saying
no.
but I cannot tell which body,
no.

Our fingers are leaving marks in each other's skin
where we clutch,
unmoving, yet sinking deeper.

I remember
shortness of breath,
no
and fogging windows,
no.

With our burning hands pressing against sweat,
in retrospect
I forget if I inflicted or received the brand.

Why don't you remember how it smelled
in the cracks where you grew up,
or the name of the shampoo
your grandmother made you use
that one time you got lice?

I'm in a life-raft filled with apricots
settled in the boggy bit
between two cherry trees
watching my grandmother water her rosebushes.

Cherries drop into the apricots and rot,
the air is almost repulsively sweet.

My spiders leave me,
and drown themselves
in the stream from the hose in her hand.

She and her collection of hand-painted porcelain dolls
turn their eyes to the spiders
then to me.

What a bucket.

Why won't you return to us
in the cracks where you grew up?

Nothing here has changed,
but we've found you rearranged by time.

Where did you find these cracking bits
that decorate your head and toes?

How could you trade your jet black feathers
for brittle porcelain bones?

Who poisoned all these moments
making everything seem bitter?

Do you not remember any joy?

When did you become someone
who is so afraid of touching us,
and would you please remember our names
or acknowledge the pains we went through
to bring you back?

Oh,
Old Friend,
when did we outgrow the cracks where we grew up?

Until now we had forgotten how much
it hurt to grow.

Was it when we sprouted antlers and hooves
to fend off the noises in the woods,
the bones that now knock sharp on walls,
leaving gashes in the doorways
marring where we measured the worth
of our growing pains?

I cannot choose it for you,
but this time I can't forget.

Lash me to a Catherine wheel,
roll me out the doors into the rain!

Pass me through the hall of mirrors,
I need to see what it looks like
when I cry!

Oh!
Old Friend, I think we're suffering,
but we don't even have hands.

MANY
HAPPY
ONES

CONFECTION'S CLOSE ENOUGH FOR ME

Whisk me away
make me a meringue.

Split me,
separate my insides
from my outs
and beat me until I reach a heightened state
where I can be made sweet.

TEETHING A TINTYPE

I've found my kneecaps in a bed of orchids
that have wound their roots around
my first lost tooth.

I make my knees into a locket that I place under my tongue.

There's the rustling of a photo growing inside,
it will be a picture of someone who is too comfortable
with being lost.

I remember roots being ripped up prematurely
and a crisp dollar underneath my pillow.

I get as close as I can
to putting my tooth back in my head,
and lay myself in the mouth of an orchid.

MULTIPURPOSE

Sleep, divided child,
sleep in the bed of orchids
all clapping for more morphine.

The blooms have drawn out their fingers for you
to swim in the gimlet-twisted,
hurried innocence still lingering behind your eyes.

Have you found a suitable place to rest your tongue?

If so,
sleep until the segmented prickles fade
and the violets applaud the murky sense
that they were useful.

Effort of Slowing

I've only slept in concept,
so this bed feels fairly foreign.

I've never heard a noiseless noise,
the lack of sound is like static
crackling in my ears
so loudly I can see it
rattling spiders in socket.

I've only gasped in panic
so slow breaths feel like drowning.

My nose has never slowed to smell security.

It's faint,
just barely sweet,
with three complex petals.

Red.

THE APEX

The composition of water is no longer questioned.

What two pronged shadow
paddles by to taunt me?

A double penumbra'd saint has no concerns
regarding self,
skating past into the disappearing line,
where snow teeth shred all conception of time
and the pond produces strikes like being five
and experiencing a nosebleed
upon realizing my skin and eye are reminiscent
of the shades and curves in cartoons,
self-consciousness becomes the length of my hair,
the single vein running over the bulge of my wrist
is a charm I learned must be hidden.

The composition of water is no longer questioned.

I feel coolness lapping,
running confliction along my edges
until I forget what boundaries are

between you and I,
the double shadow,
and the disappearing line.

EDGE PIECES

What exquisite corpses we are,
Old Friend.

How long have we been growing bits in total lack of context?

Our unknown past became a mass of limbs,
unsure of which piece is oldest,
no discernable genesis to this eager mass,
we two still lack memory
and knowledge of how to prune a tree
if we can't differentiate root and branch
or even see what pieces have fallen to the ground.

But we share what eyes we have.

There's a crow out there with three,
all closed but I know they must be
impossibly
green.

Another Hans Christian Andersen Tale

Her coat is currently pinfeathers,
all bumps, flecks, awkward bits
that jut out at the oddest angles
from her nearly raw
skin.

Halfway formed,
deaf,
eyes sealed.

Which might be mercy
since she doesn't have to see their stares.

They will see
when she does.

When I ask her the question,
when judgement rains,
her feathers will grow
and they will see
she's become
some kind of Angel.

GUILT AND INDIFFERENCE

Remember the years in the woods
where we spent our gasoline Summers crouching on rocks
scooping freckles from the faces of our reflections,
wearing our daisy chains
that handcuffed a bucket of dead bees to our wrists,
memorizing the canals etched into the dying trees?

When you left,
I memorized one that took me all the way to the center of the
wood
where there was a hole.

I took a worm and stuffed it down as deep as I could
and sealed it up.

I left the woods by climbing over the pile of grass clippings
in the hidden corner of my backyard,
and slipped my fingers back into the hooves
I planted when I learned
my babysitter was only five years older than me.

I left those years silently,
missing the days in the woods when we needed fingers.

Fingers are loud,
like your eyes.

BEING BINOCULAR

The softest thing,
say,
the sound of a single, distinct blink
of a dry eye,
that slightest scratching sensation
of the lens against the lid
reminds us we're alive.

THE FIRST ATTEMPT AT PARTING WAYS

We found it wailing through the foothills in the rain,
crying out that its hooves were already cloven,
and it could never close the rift
or be given more digits.

A Penrose beast with five legs and four feet,
a massive multitude of eyes, antlers, wings,
something shaped vaguely like a thumb,
other unrecognizables,
lacking the will to pass its present,
leaping between undecidable figures,
unwilling to discern what is head or tail
or is it stag

                  stag or bird

bird or me

             me or stag

stag or it

        it or bird

bird or stag

      stag or me

me or bird

    bird or it

it or me

   me or it

it or me
    me or it
it
 me
we meet.

IDEAS ARE WHEN YOUR BODY CATCHES UP TO INSTINCT

Add momentum   Adding momentum
ad infinitum
and moment by moment   made moment by moment
will pass faster   pass faster
than you can comprehend,   than you could comprehend,
until you reach   and when you reached
terminal velocity
where you can see yourself   where you saw yourself
looping back,
breezing past
someone experiencing
the present second
in memory,
while, simultaneously,
you look back,   you looked back,
everything will become   everything became
clear.

How badly we want to be you again, but I can't stay here.

Under the Influence of Confluence

Imbalance of grace,
overabundance of faces,
original sin in me and mine.

The merging of many,
a pity our minds couldn't think the way we said they did.

Blindness gives way to find
another kind of darkness harnessed in my tongue.

Please,
Old Friends,
run with me away from these boiling trees, the breezes that pass
by
to warn of the coming storms.

Run with me,
from the steaming dirt and maggots who burrow deep
in hopes they will not cook.

Run with me,
from that unchanging cloud where we could never hope to
touch
something bluer than the roses in my teeth.

Run with me,
away from our retreating sky
beneath the inverted streets
and swiftly deepening bed
of shedding bits we've been sleeping in.

Run with me,
in opposite directions
until we've lost all sense of the infection
I've been breeding in my mind,
a place that does not exist in this,
but may one day in that
and is, simply put,
the things we shouldn't be for the sake
of you and me remaining creatures who can walk.

Run,
in opposite directions
before we change our minds.

SHEDDING

LEVELING THE APEX

I don't remember learning how to speak,
but I know I did,
or else I would not have these words
for the missing chunks of myself.

Words like consonance and assonance,
and an essence of remembrance
of things I miss
like losing teeth
and making puppets from paper,
crayons,
and popsicle sticks.

Yet my vocabulary is limited
currently.

I yet have no word
for that split second of weightlessness
at the apex of the arch of a swing,
or for when I was thrown
so
high in the air,
limbs outstretched to snatch a cloud out of the sky
and never worried I wouldn't be caught.

Consonance and assonance
that essence of remembrance
of a word
for when the process of falling
was fearless.

Religion Taught Vs Religion Learned

I miss the dark, transcendent times
where salt was a pillow,
where we could taste the softness
hidden in the night air,
and it was like being birthed
by a maple leaf.

A time adjacent perfection,
when self was null,
when no purpose existed
but the infliction of the shallowest wounds to our palms,
and licking them like butterflies seeking respite at a riverbank.

That all too brief existence
where we did not need language,
where we were not twisted in the face
and sang with tongues
newly wetted
by the laughter tears of something
we had no other definition for
but God.

THE NECESSITY AND CAPACITY OF FORGETTING

Have you seen my collection of papers-
how many of them are about you?

You're lighter,
unnecessary,
yet no less important.

Where once I needed you
to exist more solidly than was fair to demand,
now I know
if you'd let me kiss the residue
of the wind produced by your fingertips
as they pass by each midnight,
I would be happy.

An Introduction to Goodbye

We've had good times here in The Parlor of Bad Behavior.

You know I abhor goodbyes
and meeting eyes for the final time,
but pop open something resembling champagne,
toast to never seeing each other again
and we'll revel in the wildness
they tried to strip from me.

I'll not have tears fog your windows,
so let's drink:
to those who think they rob you of me totally
we pity those narrow minds
who'll never find such savage purity as ours!

Who knows what sorts of memories
you'll make here in The Parlor of Bad Behavior
after I'm taken off to be civilized?

I hope they'll be so joyful as now.

Let's make one more before I'm gone.

Please, tear down this wall with me?

THE SHORTEST LINE IS A DRAIN

The swarm shoots up the rocks
and hovers in a puddle at my feet.

I beg them to show me what I might look like
in an existence that is not geodesic,
but one that winds away,
trades its left foot for a rabbit's,
skips back down the cliffs with them,
and reaches the boom
where the shudder of approaching lives
beyond our high tide twists and recedes
on waves of boiling ice.

I beg them to teach me what it might look like
to wave goodbye to the fragile grasses on the banks,
the blades that grew imperceptibly
but came to tower over my head
before I noticed them.

I'm thin,
you swarm,
my life's a line
and I must no longer be infinity in one direction.

Save me from a lack of depth,
show me how to curl in three dimensions.

Traditional Pests in Suburbia

I found a piece of my humanity buried with the mailboxes
that once lined the cul-de-sac where we grew up.

I was told to never play with my shadow
or it would become something fearful,
but I of course did,
and I heard the mutters,

Dig, kid,
Dig.

They said again to me,

Remember the sandbox
and the earwigs we buried there?

Dig, kid,
Dig.

There's a letter here
from that pen pal you always wanted!

And I found six inches deep in dirt,
a scrap of paper.

Hi,
what's your name?

SAN ANDREAS' FAULTS

The breeze knows,
oh,
how the breeze knows,
how it knows the words that worked me silently.

The breeze knows,
oh,
how the breeze knows,
how it knows the throes of time
and how they hunted me,
please
take these words back when I am gone,
rest them with my first memory of my reflection

The breeze knows,
oh how the breeze knows,
how it knows the ancients becoming new.

Through countless revolutions and turnings of the tide
your eyes remain as wide and bright as a child's.

Oh,
only the breeze,

the ancient beast
that twirls the world collecting sorrows,
knows how deeply I have missed you.

WERE-

Your dimples made me believe in demonic possession
I thank them for that.

I never had faith in anything rougher than sandpaper
until you told me
that the Devil spawns the snakes from feathers,
that I have always been an animal,
that it's not a crime to leave my skin
draped over the rafters,
and that the caterpillars crack when they smell blood.

With that,
I'll sing the song you taught me,
the one with the chorus that makes you go

ooh

that makes you smile,
and I will burn our clothes,
forget
humanity knows fire in any capacity.

And since I've learned
loss

is all I ever wanted
we can disappear,
guiltless,
back into the woods
where we will make the caterpillars crack.

SHEDDING

Red-chested
I run with abandon
back to the cracks
letting branches rip
the velvet from my antlers.

The strips cascade
and wrap around me,
slick, and stinging with joy.

My bandages of skin
make my whole body raw
and ready
to relish
my returns.

ABOUT THE AUTHOR

Rhys Daly is an Asian-American Seattle area writer and actor who wishes he lived even closer to the ocean. His work often explores discomfort, uncertainty, identity, acceptance, and the wonder in the mundane. When he's not hunched over a coffee table furiously memorizing lines or scribbling up poems, he can be found walking moodily down a city street looking for his next bit of inspiration. Other works can be in Volume Four, Issue 3 of *Rigorous Magazine*, as well as the Fall 2020 issue of *Short Vine Journal* under the name Cyan.

About the Press

Unsolicited Press based out of Portland, Oregon and focuses on the works of the unsung and underrepresented. As a womxn-owned, all-volunteer small publisher that doesn't worry about profits as much as championing exceptional literature, we have the privilege of partnering with authors skirting the fringes of the lit world. We've worked with emerging and award-winning authors such as Shann Ray, Amy Shimshon-Santo, Brook Bhagat, Kris Amos, and John W. Bateman.

Learn more at unsolicitedpress.com. Find us on twitter and instagram.